The economics of Crypto-Currency Mining

Hal Hashimoto

Pre-Alpha Edition

January 2021

Section One: In the beginning

This book is intended for all audiences and will shy away from overly technical explanations. The goal of this book is to explain why crypto-currency mining is profitable (or not), how to quantify it and to value mining operations. This is a completely new phenomenon and the beauty of it is that anyone can be a part of it. One does not need permission, expertise or technical knowledge to participate in the Bitcoin derived ecosystems. Only curiosity and resolve is necessary for success.

This book isn't a guide on how to mine, or how to get rich doing so. It isn't going to tell you which new fashionable crypto-coin or token to mine, what hardware to buy, whether to solo-mine or use a pool or how to set up mining software. It isn't going to show you how to setup a rig properly, how to modify your GPU BIOS or memory timings, how to fine tune performance and power usage or how to plug it all in. It isn't going to tell you how much money you are going to make nor try to sell you anything. It avoids specific projects, algorithms, software and hardware. Some time ago I created cryptominingtalk[1] to answer the most basic mining questions which kept popping up over and over again on the bitcointalk forum (it is outdated now), so I encourage you to take a look if you are interested. In any case the are multitudes of posts and guides out there that are easily found using a duckduckgo search. If you did not understand half of what was written above, again, do not despair for all those terms are not important at all in respect to the objectives of this book.

This book is a guide on how to value mining. How to put a price or a relative metric on different pieces of hardware and mining operations. For new miners it offers a glimpse of the way forward. For policy makers it offers a basic introduction to the industry without touching the toxic soup of misinformation that is fed daily on social media or in lobbyist meetings so that they can allocate their resources properly. For investors it will open up the idea that traditional methods of value are of little consequence in this industry. Although one can successfully compare a crypto-currency mine to a gold mine, one must compare it to a market that is much more volatile and has a rate of technological improvement that was previously unheard of. In addition, there are no longer any significant barriers to entry in the market, much expertise is now common knowledge and specialized mining tools and software are now available to all (for a fee usually). Considering the valuations and quantity of new publicly listed companies "playing" the blockchain and mining, I feel that this book is many years overdue.

The idea of the book has been fermenting slowly for three or four years as I saw events and projects unfold before me. What was previously a fringe market and a novelty for the most technologically and privacy inclined individuals has become somewhat acceptable in everyday life. It has become, it seems, the new normal. One only needs to watch CNBC to see that, apparently, buying Bitcoin is now part of a sound portfolio. Now I would call that transformation quite interesting to say the least, considering what Bitcoin really is. In this book, we will introduce basic mining concepts and talk about hardware. We will analyze how to put a valuation on that hardware and on the whole mining operation. By the end of the book, we will be able to analyze publicly listed companies and see whether they deserve their valuations or not.

Section 2: A Proper Introduction

A dream of freedom. An idea that, although a country may control local money creation (new loans), it should and could not control an individual's right to global monetary freedom and independence that transcends national borders. A dream born out of public key cryptography, the greatest achievement in the field since clay tablets were used to encrypt data in Mesopotamia thousands of years ago. That all became incorporated in Bitcoin. It is privacy and liberty for each and every one of us and it paves the way to a better future regardless of political ideologies, geographical situation or wealth.

Many have dreamed and laid the groundwork of such freedom, often in indirect ways, from Zimmermann's PGP[2] to Neil Stephenson's Cryptonomicon and to all the idealists on the now infamous Cypherpunk mailing list (just to name a few). From Chaum's Digicash to Cybercash. Satoshi Nakamoto is the name everyone knows and mentions but it is worthwhile to remember that the creator's anonymity was a requirement for the project to work.

In the beginning, there was Bitcoin. But who has the right to create Bitcoin and distribute the coins (private keys) ? Who has the authority to do so ? The answer is no one. Satoshi Nakamoto is no one. It is by design. From this point on, anyone could copy Bitcoin and create their own coins. But Bitcoin was fair, open, free and idealistic. You could store it, transfer it and it was somewhat protected and safe. In any case, the user was responsible – the user was independent and free to do as he pleased. He had no permission to ask for or receive. There was no absolute authority on nothing. No one truly in charge. There was no one to trust. The early programmers had such authority, but others were free to accept, reject and debate every single step of the way. And they did. That gave it intrinsic value and before long it also had a monetary value – a real perceived value.

So in the beginning, no one created Bitcoin. Then as soon as it was created, there was mining. For better or for worse, mining is now an industry. How this industry fares is somewhat irrelevant to Bitcoin's story, as much as Google's work is irrelevant to the overall story of the internet. People will go to great lengths to monetize anything that has value.

Our focus is mining. After the beginning, there were many coins. There were free and fair coins and many more that were not. As value was extracted, greed settled in. We had pre-mined coins (coins with a big first reward block), insta-mined coins (the first blocks were big and also impossible to actually mine), pre-sold coins (pre-mined coins actually sold before launch, such as ethereum), tokens and much, much more. Specialized hardware replaced consumer hardware and everyday a new coin was created and an other died.   And so miners navigate the choppy seas of fickle value and short term projects. They do so because it permits them to extract Bitcoin from the system. It is how miners accumulate Bitcoin. I would prefer to mine Bitcoin directly, but my ASIC BlockErupter solo hashing at 333mhs is still waiting for a block 7 years on (that is a joke. It is really solo mining though).

Section Three: Prerequisite knowledge

There are many types of mining hardware available – CPUs, GPUs, FPGAs and ASICS. There are also many altcoins with algorithms that are tailored for specific hardware. The economics of mining stay the same regardless of the coin, algorithm or hardware so we will bundle everything together. There is a difference between general purpose hardware and application specific hardware.

A graphics card can be used to play games, some may be used for machine learning calculations or graphical rendering. A CPU can be used for almost any task. An FPGA can be used in a variety of industrial applications including missile guidance technology (which is why there are restrictions on exports). An ASIC serves no purpose other than the specific application it was conceived for. If there is an algorithm change on a coin, then all the ASICs on that particular algorithm become virtually useless.

In addition, technological advances in chip manufacturing, which reduce the power used per hash and increases chip density render old ASICs useless over time. Those can be recycled but most often end up in landfills creating an environmental and sustainability problem.

On the other hand, any other hardware can be re-purposed and live a long and healthy life even if obsolete. Not every application requires the latest chip. In addition there are storage coins which use storage capacity and internet bandwidth to generate value. The economics are the same, although the hardware (Hard Disks) has a much lower power usage. The whole Bitcoin network can run on a few old computers, but it would not be a strong network. The vast amounts of energy it consumes is necessary for it to be resilient and incorruptible. The price and difficulty of bitcoin mining is what ultimately determines total hashpower and global power usage. This is also why popular talk about energy consumed per transaction is irrelevant (they are not related). The mining process is called Proof Of Work, and this was created before Bitcoin. It is part of the magic of having a system where you need not trust your counterpart for the success of a transaction.

How do we assign value to mining equipment ?

There are a few main components to calculating hardware value and profitability. Because this is a completely new field of expertise, we shall have to use novel and tailored metrics to evaluate different hardware. Although the sector is maturing, the fact remains that any investment in mining hardware is a high risk activity. That risk is ill-defined and hard to quantify, but we can assign probabilities and tolerances that will enable us to take informed decisions on our purchases.

The first factor to consider before putting an order for hardware is mining costs. There are variable costs and fixed costs. The fixed costs are the same as in any other industry – the hardware itself, rent, building setup, electricity hardware such as transformers and power distribution units, ventilation, internet, security, taxes, loan payments, etc. A nice building with the highest data center industry norms may look good on a guided investor tour but adds nothing to actual mining profitability. The savvy miner will maintain proper temperature, humidity, clean air and ease of access to the hardware with the *lowest possible fixed costs*. This point is very important and often confuses the general investing public. The focus is not on lowering fixed costs to improve profitability (although it does), the philosophy is to have costs so low that the venture can actually survive in a downturn (Of which there are many. Remember, Bitcoin always crashes). This philosophy also extends the profitability of older equipment and gives the operator more flexibility in changing market conditions.

A common myth in crypto-currency mining is that one needs a large operation with lots of capital to be profitable. That could not be further from the truth ! Take the example of a homeowner who subsidizes his mining fixed costs through his living arrangements – sacrificing a few square feet in his garage or basement for the mining rigs. His total fixed cost is equal to the mining rig's actual cost. He can buy a miner (assuming no investment needed for the electric or ventilation systems) and can simply plug it in.

In fact, the most profitable mining operation is the home miner who lives in a country where there are cool temperatures and low electric rates. He can then actually use his mining waste heat to lower or eliminate his home heating costs in the winter, and to reduce basement humidity in the summer. Such a miner can operate even with *negative returns* and still be profitable overall. As such, there are many projects from agriculture production in Nordic areas to water heating that attempt to extract value out of mining's waste product – heat. Any industry with heat requirements should consider mining operations to subsidize or eliminate the cost of providing that heat.

The knowledgeable miner, after accounting for a lean mining setup will also consider his variable costs. Electricity is by far the most important factor to consider in any mining operation. The idea of having the lowest possible electric cost is not only directly related to profitability but also to *survival*. A 2c/kwh cost is very different from a 5c/kwh or 10c/kwh cost and this will directly influence the choice of mining hardware to purchase for the mining operation.

The first metric we introduce is therefore the cost of mining. This cost is expressed as a percentage of revenue. We will use CM to represent the Cost of Mining.

$$CM = C^t / R$$

(Cost of mining = Total mining costs / Returns per unit per arbitrary time period)

These equations will be simple, but they can be made as complex as you wish depending on the parameters you need to incorporate. For the sake of simplicity we will express all monetary units in $, rather than in Bitcoin. But in the end everything should be priced in Bitcoin. The goal is to accumulate Bitcoin, not $.

Variable costs are mainly electricity expenses. Total costs include variable costs plus all fixed costs divided by unit of hashpower.

$$C^t = C^v + C^f$$

C^v = Variable cost (electricity) per day per unit of hashpower
C^f = Fixed costs per day per unit of hashpower

The Unit of hashpower can be defined as one piece of equivalent hardware. Assuming the mine has only the same hardware (for simplicity), then it is easy to define that unit of hashpower (and its return). For example, a miner wishes to buy an ASIC. He knows the hashpower expressed in hashes per second and its electricity consumption. He also knows how much that hashpower returns in the market. If a piece of hardware consumes 100 watts of electricity (which costs 10cents per kwh) and has a present day return of 0.50$ per day, his cost of mining is (assuming no fixed costs) :

$CM = C^t / R$

$CM = (C^v + C^f) / R$

$CM = ((0.1 \text{ kwh} * 24\text{hours} * 0.10\$/\text{kwh}) + 0) / (0.50\$/24\text{hrs}) = 0.48$

This miner therefore has a 48% CM. The time frame we use is a day cycle as it is usually the simplest and most effective way to display this information. Notice that if this miner paid only 3c/kwh his CM would be less than 15%. In summary, he pays half his mining revenue in variable costs.

With known revenue and consumption values we can calculate the maximum electricity cost that this miner can endure if he has no other costs.

$CM = (0.1 * 24 * x) / 0.50 = 1$

$x = 0.5 / 2.4$

Solving for x gives us a value of 0.21 cents/kwh. Notice in the equation that there are 24 hours in a day and that the revenue (0.50) is quoted per day. Therefore, at 0.21c/kwh he is not profitable. But since most miner's electricity costs are fixed and do not fluctuate with time, it can be more interesting to calculate the minimum revenue per piece of hardware that he can withstand. Assuming electricity costs is now a constant, e=0.10.

$CM = (0.1 * 24 * e) / x = 1$

Solving for x gives us a minimum revenue of 0.24 $ per day. Therefore, if a negative event happens (difficulty doubles or the price halves) that miner is now unprofitable. We could have also applied the 48% value we obtained above to the revenue number for a quick and easy calculation. Knowing the rate of difficulty increase also gives us an indication, price being constant, of when the hardware will become obsolete. This does not mean that the hardware will be in fact obsolete at that point however.

Mining revenue is more complicated to grasp. In these calculations, we always use current mining revenue. As in the projected mining rewards a miner would get today. Mining rewards are a function of mining difficulty, altcoin prices and the bitcoin price.

Mining difficulty or total network hashrate is a complicated concept to properly calculate depending on the coin's difficulty adjustment algorithm, but it is easy to understand from the miner's perspective. If the daily mining reward (block time) is to stay stable as outlined in the coin's code, then the difficulty of finding such a block must change with the total hashpower in the network. The larger the hashpower, the higher the eventual difficulty of finding a block, assuming it adjusts every block. It serves little purpose to estimate mining revenue in the future for the simple reason that it will always be an imperfect and unreliable metric. We shall see why in a few pages and how we can manage and account for this risk. Mining difficulty is notoriously hard to predict, as are crypto-currency market prices. If one can reliably predict Bitcoin or altcoin prices, then it would be a much more profitable venture to become a trader, not a miner.

Coins generated per day = (Miner's Hashpower / total network hashpower) * Block rewards per day

This is an overly simplified (and incorrect) way to calculate mining rewards (which ignores many variables such as luck distribution, latency, node distribution, etc), but the idea behind the equation is simple. Everything else being equal, your hashpower in relation to the overall hashpower is directly related to the reward you get relative to the overall reward available. A shared pie, so to speak.

Of course difficulty is dynamic, block times vary, rewards per block change over time, etc. You can do the proper calculation yourself or use one of the many websites which do it for you. Remember we are not factoring in future difficulty or reward changes into the calculation. What we need to know is as of this moment, how much does this unit of hashpower make in revenue per day. A popular site to calculate this is whattomine[3] and for more information on difficulty, rewards and algorithms the bitcoin wiki[4] is very well written. Simple duckduckgo searches can answer most, if not all, technical questions on the subject.

What is important is the total cost of mining per unit of hashpower. Once all the expenses are calculated – building, wages, security, internet, ventilation costs, electricity costs not directly related to the mining hardware, etc – and divided by the total projected or actual hashpower units, we can start to make some informed and intelligent hardware decisions. Which is the point of the whole exercise. Once we understand how to value hardware, we can start to understand how to value a mining operation.

Is it a good idea to buy old, inexpensive, soon to be obsolete hardware with a high power consumption profile but with a very low upfront capital requirement ? Or an expensive upfront cost for low power consumption hardware that may last for many years ? Should the informed miner buy a CPU, GPU, FPGA, ASIC ? An AMD RX570 graphics card, or the new 5700 series ? Nvidia ? The latest version of the Antminer by Bitmain Tech or the second latest ? FPGA'S ? CPUs ? That decision is a personal one and there is no right or wrong answer. There is simply the most logical answer for the situation that the miner is in. In general, the lower your electric costs the more appealing it is to have older hardware as you can maximize your hashpower for less capital (assuming you have the space and power capacity). If you have high electric costs, then newer power efficient hardware would be more profitable over the long term. Now that we know how to calculate our actual cost of mining we can introduce new metrics to value mining hardware. Remember that the Cost of Mining is always expressed as a percentage of revenue.

Two metrics that are very useful to use when deciding which piece of hardware to buy is the cost per hash and the energy consumption per hash ratios.

3   https://www.whattomine.com

4   https://en.bitcoin.it/wiki/Difficulty

$Cost^H = Cost / Hashrate$

$Cost^E = Electricity\ in\ kw / hashrate$

$Cost^H$ and $Cost^E$ are very useful when comparing mining equipment. For example we can compare two different generations of GPU mining hardware. The previous generation of AMD graphics cards includes the RX570, which can hash Dagger-Hashimoto (Ethereum) at 32mhs using 100 watts of power. The latest GPU which is based on 7nm architecture (vs 14nm), is the RX5700. This GPU has a hashrate of 55mhs and uses 125 watts.

RX570 $Cost^H = 80\$ / 32 = 2.50\ \$/mhs$
            $Cost^E = 100w / 32 = 3.13\ w/mhs$

RX5700 $Cost^H = 350\$ / 55 = 6.36\ \$/mhs$
            $Cost^E = 125w / 55 = 2.27\ w/mhs$

In addition, these GPUs are usually grouped together into "rigs". For the example, we will assume a mining rig has 6 GPUs, although that number can be much higher. A mining rig consists of an adequate power supply, a frame to hold the hardware, a motherboard, cpu, ram, hard disk and risers (these allow for a proper layout of GPU's which no longer need to be physically touching the motherboard). For an ASIC the only hardware required would be a power supply and a rack/frame. In addition to the rig, there are usually PDU's (power distribution units, similar to a common power bar) that route the power to the breaker box.

If the total cost of a rig is 350$ without the GPUs, we can update our calculation. For a 6 GPU rig the total cost per hardrate unit is :

RX570 $= 350 + (6*100\$) / 32 * 6 = 4.95\ \$/mhs$

RX5700 $= 350 + (6*350\$) / 55 * 6 = 7.42\ \$/mhs$

The RX570 6 GPU rig costs a third less per mhs vs the RX5700 rig. We can also see its very worthwhile to increase the number of GPUs per rig, especially older cheaper hardware. With an estimate of Bitcoin's future price probabilities and difficulty probabilities, you can assign a value to the hardware's resilience. How long can I mine at a profit and under what price and difficulty conditions ?

Another interesting concept in mining is "ROI". It is a mining specific term, meaning either a vague form of "return on investment" or as I prefer "return on initial". ROI is quite useful for comparing mining hardware but it must not be confused with the common financial term. ROI is measured not in percentage, but in time (days, months, years). It measures, all else being equal, the time to recover the initial investment in a piece of hardware, or a rig (or a mine).

ROI = Hardware Cost / Mining Profit per time period

Assuming constant difficulty and price, ROI tells us how many days to break even. Lets calculate ROI for our two GPUs, the RX570 and the RX5700. Accounting for variable costs (electricity at 0.10c/kwh) we assume an ROI of :

RX570 ROI = 80$ / 0.35$/day = 229 days
RX5700 ROI = 350$ / 0.72$/day = 486 days

See how this calculation changes when our savvy miner secures 3cents/kwh power :

RX570 ROI = 80 / 0.52 = 154 days
RX5700 ROI = 350 / 0.95 = 368 days

If the coin price doubles, then overnight ROI time is reduced by half. ROI does not project returns into the future, it simply evaluates *at this moment in time, all else being equal, the relative profitability of mining hardware.*

The interested reader now has a few metrics to evaluate mining hardware. So what should the cost of mining be for a healthy operation ? The real question to ask is : at what bitcoin price do I have to stop mining ? Once you find that number you can analyze whether adjustments need to be made so that the mine stays in your financial comfort zone. In general, older mining gear paired with very cheap electricity has always been the most profitable way to mine for it maximizes total hashpower for a set amount of capital. As variable / power costs rise relative to other miners costs, old gear quickly loses its appeal and its profitability.

To visualize difficulty and profitability, we can clearly see from these charts that mining is a very dynamic business (taken from bitinfocharts.com).

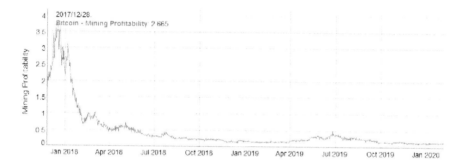

Profitability spikes always follow the coin's price because it takes some time for the miners to increase hashrate and for the difficulty to adapt. Bitcoin's profitability per unit of hashpower always goes down due to new and improved chips (with decreasing marginal improvements over time). We can say the same for Ethereum although the life cycle of a GPU is much longer and improvements much less rapid and drastic (Although there are ASICs now). A miner investing at one of those peaks with high costs will find that his mine is no longer profitable within weeks or months.

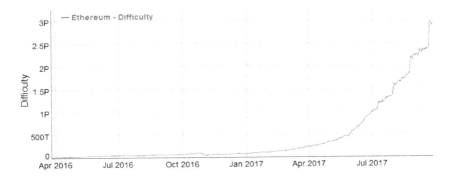

*Go see updated difficulty and hashrate charts (etherscan.io/chart/hashrate)

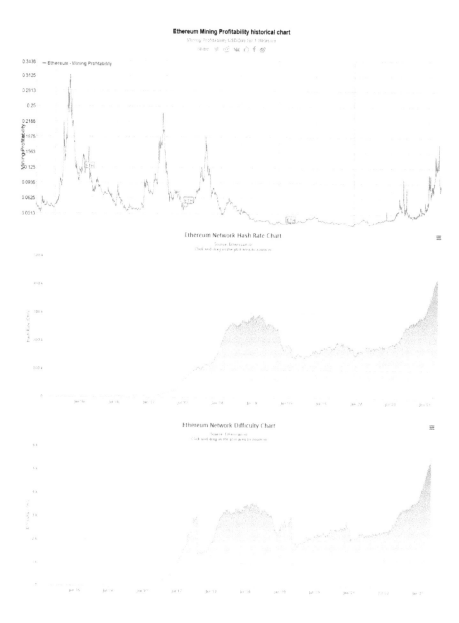

Ethereum Mining Profitability historical chart

Ethereum Network Hash Rate Chart

Ethereum Network Difficulty Chart

See how transaction fees are important for mining rewards :

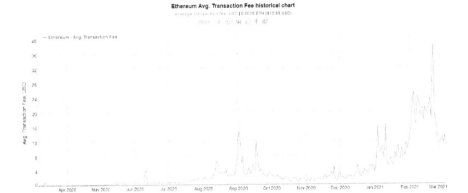

Ethereum Avg. Transaction Fee historical chart

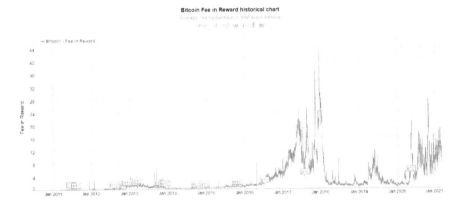

Bitcoin Fee in Reward historical chart

Bitcoin difficulty is exponential due to mining hardware improvements. For Ethereum it represents mainly the surge in new miners (except for recently – influx of ASICs). Millions of GPUs were added to the total hashpower. Looking at 2013, 2017 and 2020 :

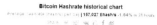

Bitcoin Hashrate historical chart

Bitcoin Hashrate historical chart

With these charts, I hope the reader gets a sense of why resilience and low costs are important factors in mining. The barriers to entry have never been lower. What was overly complicated and obscure became widely available and plug and play.

Mining profitability, all else being equal, tends to equal the network's marginal mining cost over time. That is, the cost of running one extra unit of hashpower. If there is a profit to be had, users will add hashpower until the increase in profit is equal to the added cost of that hashpower. In practice, however, things are more dynamic and can stay more profitable for a longer period of time. Network fees also play a big part in total rewards. When these are high for an extended period and hashrate increases, the profitability crash can be rapid and drastic.

Take into consideration for a moment the question that every new miner has asked : "Is mining profitable ?". The reply that comes up, whether you are in 2013 or 2020, is invariably "Mining isn't profitable". Its an interesting answer considering the rise in difficulty and thus hashing capacity since the early days of mining. Part of the answer comes from the fact that all miners share the same "meal". If you encourage others to mine that will come at your expense. Unfortunately that is a short-sighted argument.

New miners become active users and usually engage in the virtual communities they are in. New miners seek outlets for their coins and bring in new users as well. Growth in new miners means growth in the crypto ecosystem – growth in demand – which leads to price appreciation over time. Price appreciation and network fees will almost always exceed difficulty adjustments. As Bitcoin's supply has a decreasing rate of inflation over time and coins are lost or hoarded its market price will go up in the long term assuming a minimum of constant demand, increasing mining profitability. Also its harm is limited considering these are mostly small home miners who treat crypto as their new hobby. What is damaging for profitability is hardware, services and software specifically designed for mining farms that enable fast and cheap growth, for a percentage of course.

The real answer to the question "is mining profitable ?" is of course "Don't trust, verify".

Putting it all together

Since a GPU warranty usually lasts 2-3 years and after that time period there is probable hardware degradation we should amortize equipment on 3-5 years. Although a well maintained mine can have quality hardware running continuously for 3+ years without ever needing to replace parts.

A poorly managed mine will have to deal with constant part (such as GPU fans) replacements after as little as one year of operation. Well under 5% of all hardware should need servicing after 2-3 years if properly operated, depending on the type and quality of hardware purchased. ASICS can have massive and catastrophic depreciation.

Knowing the cost per hashrate and all variable costs, the miner can thus decide which hardware to buy. Knowing that the business is volatile and dynamic, he opts for the lowest possible fixed costs.

For the financial analyst, evaluating an existing mining operation is quite difficult. Traditional metrics and financial reports are unfortunately of little use to have an accurate picture of the whole operation. Management's strategy is what determines profit in the long term, so it is wise to evaluate mining firms based on the competence and knowledge of the management team. Knowing how to value equipment and how to operate a mine can enable the intelligent analyst to spot red flags : overpriced or unnecessary equipment, high fixed costs, dubious GPU hardware choices when alternatives are available with much better ROI, Cost to hash ratios, inadequate ventilation and usage of space, non-optimized hardware (a stock RX570 may hash 30-40% less for 30-40% more power vs optimized), large payrolls or number of employees, among others. Once the mine has a track record, he can use traditional methods of evaluating the business but must keep in mind that even perhaps Cobalt mining in the Democratic republic of the Congo may have less risk than running a bitcoin mine. Knowing break even metrics, minimum bitcoin price and maximum difficulty adjustments can help establish a probabilistic profit analysis.

Imagine a mine that is unprofitable under a 5000$ Bitcoin price, or is deemed unprofitable if difficulty increases by a set amount. If It is thought that the odds of a drop in half of the price in bitcoin is 25%, and a positive breakout at 25% would triple profits, then we can say:

Next Year Projected Returns = ((ProbDrop * Returns(0)) + (ProbStable * Returns(1))
$\qquad$ + (ProbHigh * Returns(3)))

Next Year Projected Returns = $0 + 0.50 + 0.75 = 1.25$

This indicates a positive outlook for mine returns. We can then say that, for example, we assume difficulty to double this year with 50% certainty, to triple with 25% chance and to stagnate with another 25%.

Next Year Projected Returns = $((1.25*0.50)*0.50) + (1.25*0.33)*0.25 + (1.25*0.25)$

Next Year Projected Returns = $0.3125 + 0.103 + 0.3125 = 0.728$

By having these numbers we can now fully evaluate a Bitcoin mine into the future based of course on a large number of assumptions. It is notoriously hard to estimate difficulty and price. But we can assign probabilities that are based on historical data and common sense (or generally accepted data) and use those to extrapolate returns to base our investment decisions on. In this case, after one year we expect the mine to, on average of all probabilities, return 27.2% less than this year.

Inputs can be adjusted in a dynamic fashion and we can infer from the change and the rate of change in the next year's projected return if our outlook is getting better or worse, and how fast.

The following questions can now be answered and a suitable answer to the question "Is mining profitable ?" can be found.

- What are the fixed costs ?
- What are the variable costs ?
- What is the Cost to Hash at the available variable and total cost adjusted price ?
- What is the price and difficulty that renders the operation unprofitable ?
- What is the probabilistic next year projected return adjusted for price and difficulty value ?
- And the years after ? What is the rate of change and what is the estimated profitable lifespan of the mine ?
- What is the management's strategy ? Mine and hold all coins minus expenses ? Active trading, selling all coins daily, investment in altcoins, constant reinvestment and expansion ? (An optimal strategy seems to be to accumulate in periods of price stagnation and to sell the crypto in periods of rapid price appreciation – this also requires « faith »). A mining operation is thus also a investment/trading operation by its nature, unless it sells all its rewards the moment it creates them.

Dynamics of crypto-currency profitability

When the price rises, people pile into mining at irrational rates. They pay irrational prices for hardware and have unrealistic expectations. This increases difficulty (every unit of hashpower added - even to your own mine, all else being equal, decreases profitability of all existing units of hashpower) which reduces profitability. That increases the cost of mining. And so on until the people with the highest total mining costs per hash shut down their operations.

At first, the big operations with salaries to pay, security, big data center buildings (expensive fixed costs) suffer. Those with low fixed costs but high electricity prices also suffer first. Difficulty stops rising but it is not enough. Soon those with medium power costs are struggling. People start selling hardware. Over leveraged miners sell coin as the price goes down. The negative feedback loop intensifies until people actually drop out and quit. Mining hardware is sold at rock bottom prices, difficulty goes down and profits recover somewhat. People with very low variable costs buy that hardware, which increases hashrate thus stabilizing difficulty.

In every scenario, a high cost operation fails. It is up to each miner to do his homework. What minimum size mine can I operate and have a decent total cost of mining ? Maximum ?
What hardware is available to me and at what prices ? How do I reduce my cost per unit of hashpower (more GPUs per rig, older GPUs). Do I have capacity constraints? Does that warrant putting priority on maximum hashrate vs cost-effectiveness?

What are my variable costs ? How do I reduce them or adjust if they are too high ? (newer GPUs, power efficient hardware, renewable energy setup, recycle and reuse waste heat)

How do I reduce my fixed costs ? Modular cheap hardware housing for example. See picture for Bitmain Tech's installations and Genesis Mining GPU's.

Enigma Mine / Ethereum Farm Buildout
www.genesis-mining.com

General thoughts for decision makers

As a rule of thumb, mining is very electricity intensive. It is also very volatile. A large farm running older hardware can shut off at any time and the owners may leave everything on site and disappear with bills unpaid. That is because the value of the hardware they have can go down to insignificant amounts. Power theft is appealing because of the potential gain and little risk. There are stories of power chip fraud in electronic power meters an of course « old school » electricity theft. In addition, there is absolutely no real job creation in a mining operation relative to the amounts of money involved. In fact, if we look at jobs created per dollar invested or per kwh consumed we can estimate that mining is one of the worst, if not the worst energy intensive industry of them all.

In Quebec, Canada where power is cheap and plentiful, expectations have been smashed. Projected demand for power surged to baffling GigaWatt numbers during the 2017 run. Actual power delivered years later was only a mere fraction of that. Still, the province has interesting power costs and attracts major data center operators. To decide which projects get subsidized power contracts, they (as bureaucrats often do) created a point system to evaluate projects. But instead of actually evaluating profitability and resilience they have what we can call a social score. The idea is simple but fundamentally misguided. For example, they favor operations that create jobs for the community.

But as we now understand, a mining operation creates no such jobs – no matter the size. A mining operation also has absolutely no research and development expenses. Any significant job and investment numbers that the state owned company has received are at best wishful thinking and at worst outright fraud. A mining software company needs no cheap electricity. Neither does a chip design company. Neither does a mining pool operator. They need a cheap and qualified labor pool and an industrial hub to prosper.

A mining operation is most profitable over the medium-long term if it can keep all its costs down to a minimum in respect to other players in the market. Plentiful high paying jobs with large research and development budgets are not only at odds with this, they are incompatible. A vertically integrated company like Bitmain Tech is different - it designs its own chips (but manufactured by TSMC or others), has its own mining operations, sells mining hardware around the world, operates popular mining pools/software and is involved in large amounts of research and development.

Analysis time

This chapter will focus on actual mining companies which are listed on stock exchanges. Public companies have strict requirement in regards to financial reporting and investor guidance. Let's see if those numbers make sense and if they are being honest about guidance. We can source all information on the SEDAR/EDGAR for Canada/USA for any publicly listed firm.

Hive Blockchain Technologies Ltd is a canadian based company, currently valued at almost 2 billion dollars (Feb 2021). This company has ordered 3000 extra BTC ASICs and expects them to be installed/received by april 2021. They immediatly state that the COVID-19 pandemic has impacted supply chains from Asia. This is a bad start as far as investor guidance is concerned and a gross understatement. Although their orders may be filled and received on time, the world is currently undergoing a massive chip shortage, even leading major car manufacturers to idle plants. This is not cause by the pandemic, although it doesn't help. It is caused by a variety of factors, including chip yields, massive demand from popular product cycles (game consoles, etc) and the fact that chip manufacture is capital intensive and cannot be expanded rapidly.

Assuming everything goes well and they receive equipment on time, we know they will have 1.673 EH/s BTC mining capacity this year. They also expect shipments of 8GB GPUs. They also report 65 million cash and coins on hand. They are also issuing new shares on the stock market, up to 100$million dollars.

Since they are paying 8.75$USD million for 8GB gpus, expanding MW usage by 30% to a total of 6MW we can deduct some information. A typical new gen GPU generates (as an example using rough numbers) 0.40 mh/s per watt. 2 000 000 watts therefore equals 800 000mh/s which translates to about 14 500 (again roughly) equivalent RX5700 GPUs. The price therefore paid per GPU is equal to 600$USD per GPU. This is 50% higher than its actual MSRP. Of course, considering the current chip shortage, GPU shortage, this is the prevailing market price. But it does fit in with what we have discussed in the first part of the book.

We can assume that the remainder of the 4MW is older POLARIS type GPUs, which roughly fetch 0.28 mh/s per watt. This equals to an RX470 equivalent of 37 000 GPUs. Not a bad mine, considering 37 000 RX470s and 14 500 RX5700s (equivalents). Add to that 1.673 EH/s so 15 000 equivalent new gen ASICs.

If we look at Q2 2020, they generated 32 800 ETH, 88 300 ETC and 89 BTC. We won't discuss the actual financial reporting as it is, in fact, quite irrelevant. We already have all the numbers we need. We can expect them to mine (at full capacity, which is only projected) at current elevated rewards a total of 200 000 USD for the GPU mining operation per day, and 600 000 USD with the BTC mining operation. This totals 800 000 USD per day, or rougly 300 million USD per year. The total mining electricity consumption is almost 60 MW. In fact, since most of the BTC hashrate is from an older generation of hardware, the actual electricity consumption would be higher. In any case, we can look at our numbers.

Have fun plugging the numbers in the equations from the first part of the book. With very generous assumptions, we can say they have a 5% cost of electricity relative to mining operations, so 40 000$ a day. They also have debt, employees, buildings, fixed costs, security, transaction fees, etc. Assuming their variable costs run about 15 million USD a year and a lower amount for all other costs, we can immediatly see this is a very profitable endevour. What if profitability goes back to what it was 8 months ago? A 10% cost of mining becomes 45%. Oh. What? Let's look at the mechanisms at work.

Assuming total costs of 20 million and revenue of 300 million a year (again, extropolating from SEDAR reporting and making generous assumptions), we have a cost of mining at a rate of 7%. Which is quite phenominal for a mine. Looking at ETH mining hashrate etherscan.io/chart/hashrate and BTC blockchain.com/charts/hash-rate, we can obviously see rapid rise in mining popularity.

I don't recall seeing in the financial reporting of the company a notice that says that each additional hash generated by the same company reduces its current hash stock's profitability (all else being equal), but it is true. If we look at the prices (cryptowat.ch/charts/KRAKEN:BTC-USD) and ETH-USD, is is quite obvious we have been going through a rapid price appreciation. If prices fall to what they were less than a year ago, say divided by 4 which is not unreasonable, then the cost of mining goes up to 30%. But the difficulty continues to rise for some time due to massive orders of gear that takes time to arrive and be installed (see projected increase in hashrate for this company). That is also negative news.

When we take into account total compensation packages in the mix if we are to analyze the stock price, the total aggregated cost of mining shoots up significantly. Stock options and share grants dilute shareholders, as do secondary share offerings. Looking at generous numbers, we see 280 million dollar profits that can vary all the way down to 50 million. The upside is rather limited for an investor for various reasons. Mainly it would be due to an increase in the price of crypto. Therefore, as people usually say in a bull market - it is always better to buy crypto than to mine. What that means is that if you buy gear at 50% or more over MSRP you may find that expected returns do not materialize as we have seen in the previous bitcoin and altcoin pumps. It is a long term bull run but with vicious short term fluctuations.

So at best this company is valued at 7 times annual mining rewards, and at the other end of the spectrum it can be valued at 35 times annual mining rewards assuming a price correction. Even at best, 7 times mining rewards it is a strech. That would mean, for a home miner, that his RX5700 (which makes 1700$ a year at current elevated prices) is valued at 14 000$. An average home mine with 50 GPUs thus would be valued at 620 500 $. That would equal a valuation that is 25x initial capital costs. This is only rational if the market doesn't understand mining difficulty, or expects a large increase in rewards. This is not financial advice, but a rational analysis of numbers extrapolated from public filings made with many asumptions. Feel free to run your own numbers and come to your own conclusions. Of course, if the price of crypto assets keep going up for a long period of time, then all mines become profitable. Price is everything.

www.ingramcontent.com/pod-product-compliance
Lightning Source LLC
Chambersburg PA
CBHW061059050326
40690CB00012B/2674